CONTENTS

INTRODUCTION

If you happen to know a child (or an adult!) who loves all things Jurassic, then this book is the perfect way to keep them entertained with 15 easy dinosaur-themed craft activities. These include dressing-up projects, like the T. rex head mask and stomping dinosaur paws; toy projects, such as the magnetic pencil case and mini Jurassic land; and decor projects, including a wonderfully flumpy snugglesaurus cushion. There's also a section on how to throw the ultimate prehistoric party, with ideas for dinosaur-themed games, decorations, and nibbles, plus an erupting volcano cake.

All the projects in this book are broken down into easy-to-follow instructions with photographed steps to guide you along. Craft materials are clearly listed at the beginning of each project.

The level of involvement for children will of course depend on their age, but we have ensured that each project has something they can all get involved with. Many of them have been designed for children to make with only a little adult assistance, such as the fossils, peg puppets, and footprint stamps. It's great to let your child lead a craft project as much as they can, to get a more personal result that they will love so much more. They may not be able to operate a sewing machine of course, but they will love to sit on your knee, press the buttons, and help guide the fabric.

Happy crafting!

TOOLS AND MATERIALS

You don't need tons of craft stuff to get creative. All the projects in this book use materials that you probably already have at home or are able to get hold of easily. Here is an overview of the materials and supplies that are really useful for the projects in this book and for crafting with kids in general.

Sewing supplies

- **Felt** is the best material for sewing with kids. It's easy to work with, doesn't fray, plus it's cheap and colorful.

- **Fleece** is another great fabric that doesn't fray. It is soft and snuggly, and perfect for costumes and larger projects.

- **A sewing machine** is not essential, but it's a good time saver. The cape and cushion do really require one. You don't need to be an expert to use one, but if you need some tips there are some fantastic tutorials online to get you started.

Craft essentials

- **Permanent colored markers** are great for adding stay-on color without having to dig out the paints. Obviously you need to take care with kids as they will treat these pens like felt tips and if you turn your back you may find your child has tattooed the baby or created their own mural!

- **Craft foam** is a durable and waterproof alternative to card stock and a fantastic thing to have around for kids' crafting in general.

- **Double-sided tape** is a no-mess, instant way to stick and a child-friendly alternative to glue. You can get really strong varieties that will stick anything.

- **Acrylic paints** add strong, permanent color to projects, but they are not the most child-friendly paints available. If children are using them they must of course be supervised, with clothes and surfaces protected. You can use child-friendly paints instead, but bear in mind the end result probably won't last as well.

- **Soft polymer clays,** such as Fimo and Sculpey, are great for children and perfect for small items like jewelry. **Air-dry clay** is cheaper, really easy to use, and can be painted once dry.

- **Shrink plastic** is a wonderful product for kids to play with. Everyone loves seeing their creations curl up and shrink to a tenth of their size once they've been in the oven. The finished result is strong and durable.

Get a craft rummage box

Find a large box and gradually fill it with old cartons, lids, card, fabric scraps, and anything else you think has an interesting shape or color. Kids love having a craft box to rummage through, and you might be surprised at the amazing things they can produce when left to their own devices with a box of materials, some tape, and a smidge of glitter.

DINOSAUR PAWS

Become a stomping T. rex with these dinosaur paws. Spray paint is best for this project as it gives great coverage, but you could use normal paint if you prefer. Bear in mind the foam tends to absorb the paint and the result may be a little patchy. Wear your paws with the cape on page 20 for a total prehistoric transformation!

You will need

- 30 x 20in (75 x 50cm) of upholstery foam, 2in (5cm) thick
- 14 x 10in (35 x 25cm) of upholstery foam, 1in (2.5cm) thick
- Pen or pencil
- Sharp knife or craft knife
- Sewing pins
- Embroidery thread
- Plastic sewing needle
- Sheets of newspaper
- Green spray paint
- Scraps of black craft foam
- Black duct tape
- Strong glue

You could paint your dinosaur paws to match your favorite dino toy.

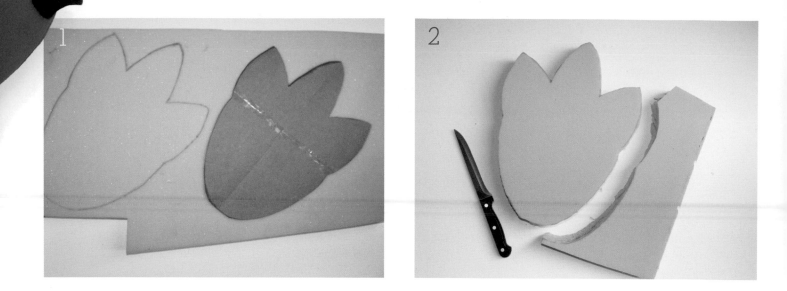

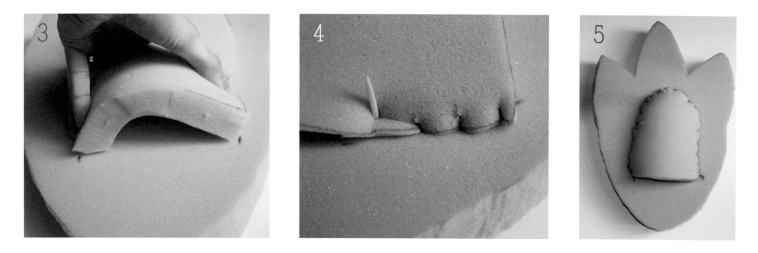

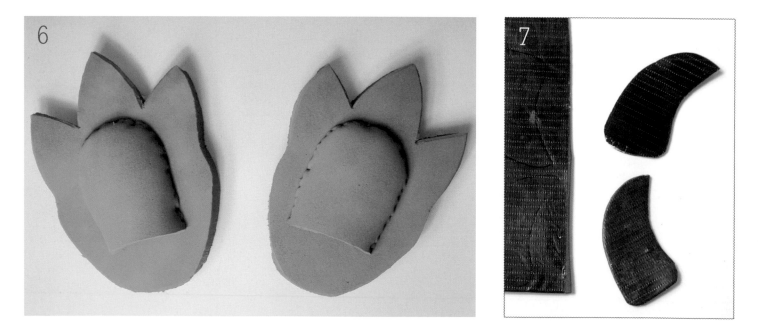

Step 1

Use the templates on page 62 for the Dinosaur Paws. Draw the shape of two paws onto the thicker foam. Use the template of the foot cover to draw two of them onto the thinner foam.

Step 2

Use a sharp knife or craft knife to cut out each paw and foot cover. An adult should do this.

Step 3

Take one of the foot covers and place in the center of the paw, with the rounded edge just under the toes. Squeeze the sides together so the foam forms a slight arch. Push pins into the foam to hold in place. Repeat for the other paw.

Step 4

Starting at one corner of each foot cover, use embroidery thread and a large plastic needle to sew the foam together (approximately ½in/1cm from the edge of the cover). Push the needle through to the base of the paw and pull taut for each stitch.

Step 5

Repeat all the way round to the other corner, leaving the flat edge open. Secure with a knot on the underside of the paw.

Step 6

Lay out some newspaper on the ground outside (or in a well-ventilated area) and ask an adult to spray the top and sides of the paws with green paint. Leave to dry.

Step 7

Cover one side of the black craft foam with black duct tape. Use the template on page 62 to draw six claws onto the back of the foam. Turn the template over so that two of the claws are facing the other direction.

Step 8

Glue the claws onto the ends of the toes.

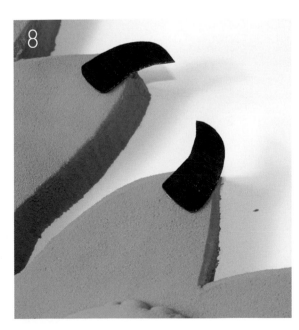

PTERODACTYL WINGS

These fabric pterodactyl wings, which are attached to the wrists with elastic, are great fun to flap around in and they're really easy to make. If you don't have a sewing machine, you could glue the fabric scales in place using fabric glue.

You will need

- Tape measure
- 1yd (1m) of orange cotton fabric
- Scissors
- Iron and ironing board
- 2yd (2m) of light-weight fusible interfacing
- ½yd (0.5m) each of yellow, orange, and brown cotton fabrics
- Sewing pins
- Sewing machine and matching thread (or fabric glue)
- 1yd (1m) of 1in (2.5cm)-wide orange bias tape
- Sewing needle and thread
- 1yd (1m) of ½in (1cm)-wide yellow elastic

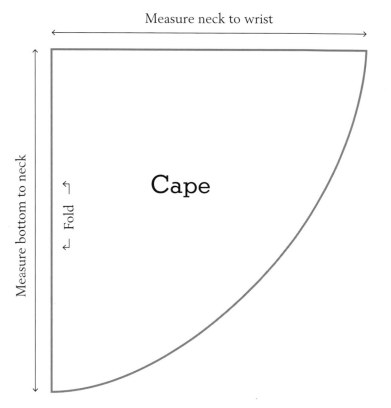

Measure neck to wrist

Measure bottom to neck

↑ Fold ↩

Cape

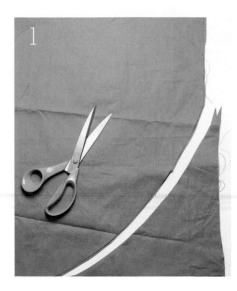 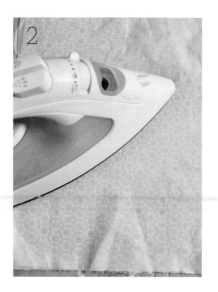 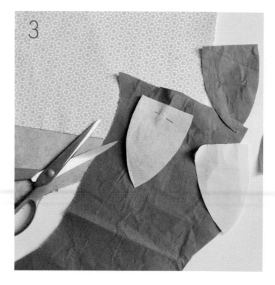

Step 1

Ask an adult to help measure you. Measure the distance between your neck and the top of your legs. Then measure from your neck to your wrist. Fold the large piece of orange fabric in half and use the measurements together with the cape diagram on page 8 to cut the piece of orange fabric.

Step 2

Following the manufacturer's instructions, iron the interfacing onto the back of the smaller pieces of yellow, orange, and brown fabrics.

Step 3

Use the template on the right to cut out scales from the interfaced fabrics.

Step 4

Cut out approximately 100 of these scales from the interfaced fabric.

Step 5

Starting at the bottom of the orange fabric, pin the scales on in a random color order. The scales should hang down from the bottom and cover the fabric underneath. Add another row on top, overlapping the first row. Keep going until all the orange fabric is covered.

Step 6

Using the sewing machine, sew along the straight edge of each scale with a ¼in (5mm) seam allowance. You will need to lift the overlapping scales out of the way as you go.

Step 7

Fold the orange bias tape over the top of the wings. Pin and sew in place. Cut away the excess bias tape.

Step 8

Cut two pieces of elastic measuring 8in (20cm) and two measuring 12in (30cm). Fold the shorter pieces in half and pin 2in (5cm) from each end of the wings for wrist straps. Hand stitch the wrist straps in place.

Step 9

Mark 4in (10cm) either side of the middle of the wings. Lay the two longer pieces of elastic out at these points, fold each end in by ¼in (5mm) and hand sew in place to create shoulder straps.

Scale
Copy at 200%

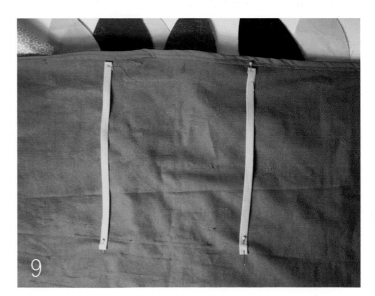

DINO FOSSILS

Create your own dig for mini paleontologists with these dinosaur fossils. They're really easy to make using a few toy dinosaurs. You can then hide them around the house or garden to be hunted and excavated by little fossil hunters. The quantities here make four fossils.

You will need

- 14–18oz (400–500g) modeling dough, such as Play-Doh
- Selection of plastic dinosaurs in various sizes
- Scissors
- 1 x sheet of acetate, about 8 x 12in (20 x 30cm)
- Sticky tape
- 7fl oz (200ml) water
- 9oz (250g) plaster of Paris
- Mixing pot

- Wooden skewer
- Tray
- Old toothbrush
- Sandpaper
- Gold and beige paint

Step 1

Roll out four balls of dough into four circles measuring about 1in (2.5cm) thick. Make sure the circles are wider than your dinosaurs. Press the dinosaurs gently into the dough to make an imprint. You can print the whole dinosaur or just the footprints or spines, if you prefer.

Step 2

Cut along the length of the acetate to make four evenly sized strips. Form them into circles that are just large enough to go around the dinosaur prints and tape the ends together. Press firmly into the dough to create a "wall" around the imprints.

Step 3

Place the dough molds onto a tray. Mix the water and plaster of Paris together in a pot with a wooden skewer. Make sure there are no lumps, then gently pour to distribute the plaster into the four molds. Give the tray a tap to remove any air bubbles from the plaster, then set aside to dry overnight.

Step 4

Gently peel the acetate sheets off the plaster and remove the dough. If the dough residue is very sticky you can leave it to dry for a bit, then rub away with a dry brush (an old toothbrush works really well).

Step 5

Sand the edges of the plaster down with sandpaper.

Step 6

Mix a little bit of beige paint with some gold to give it a slight shine. This will help pick out the contours of the dinosaurs. Paint the fossils with the mixed paint and leave to dry. Then you can have fun by hiding them in the soil or sand outside.

Plaster of Paris heats up as it hardens so an adult should always do the mixing and pouring. Never put in contact with skin.

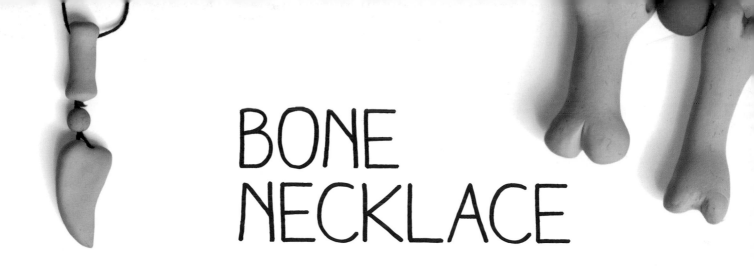

BONE NECKLACE

Wear this polymer clay bone necklace to give any prehistoric outfit the wow factor. You don't have to stick to necklaces; you could make bracelets or keyrings too using the same technique.

You will need

- 1oz (25g) of beige polymer clay
- Blunt knife
- Wooden skewer
- 1oz (25g) of red polymer clay
- 1oz (25g) of turquoise polymer clay
- Parchment paper
- Embroidery thread
- Needle
- Magnetic jewelry clasp

1

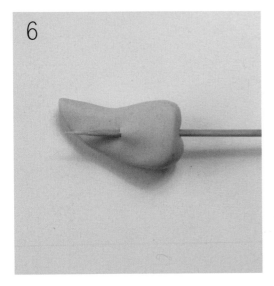

2

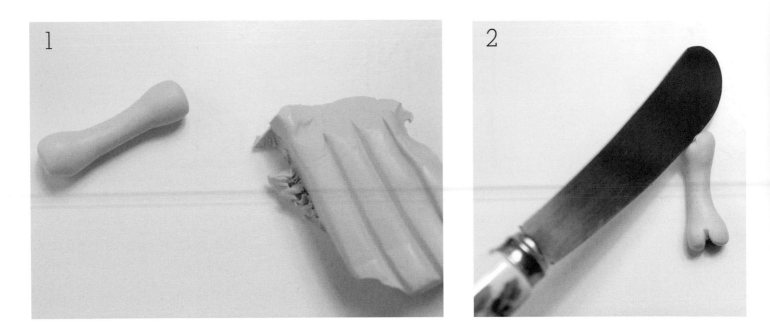

3

4

5

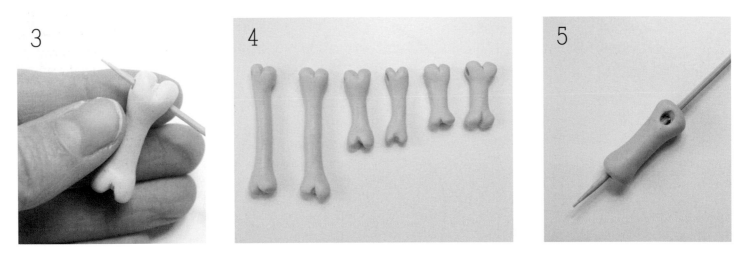

6

7

Step 1

Roll a sausage from beige polymer clay, measuring about 1½ x ½in (4 x 1cm). Pinch and roll it in the center to create a dumbbell shape.

Step 2

Use a blunt knife to press into the top of each end. Push down and wiggle the knife to create two nobbles to resemble a bone.

Step 3

Push and twist a wooden skewer through one end, using your fingers to keep the clay stable. Twist the stick and move it around a little to make the hole a bit larger. Bear in mind that thread needs to fit through it later.

Step 4

Repeat to create another bone the same size. Then make two bones from lengths of clay that are about 2in (5cm), and two that are 1in (2.5cm).

Step 5

Make another 1in (2.5cm) dumbbell shape. Push a hole through the top as before, then push another hole down the length of the clay. Twist the skewer as before to enlarge the hole.

Step 6

For the tooth, take a grape-size lump of beige clay and mold it into a triangle. Press and bend the clay until it resembles a sharp tooth. Push the wooden skewer through the top and out near the bottom of the tooth at the back, so that the hole is at an angle, as shown.

Step 7

Roll two balls the size of blueberries from the red clay and push the skewer through to turn them into beads. Repeat to create two more a little smaller, then two more, smaller still. Make three small turquoise beads in the same way. Bake the clay in the oven on parchment paper, following the manufacturer's instructions.

Step 8

To make the central pendant, thread the tooth onto an 8in (20cm) length of embroidery thread. Pull the thread round the back of the tooth and add a blue bead over both ends to secure the tooth at the bottom. Add the double-holed bone, then tie at the top with a little excess to allow you to thread the pendant to the main necklace.

Step 9

Cut a 22in (55cm) length of thread and add the beads and central pendant. Hang the necklace around the neck and adjust the length as preferred, then tie the magnetic clasp onto each end of the thread.

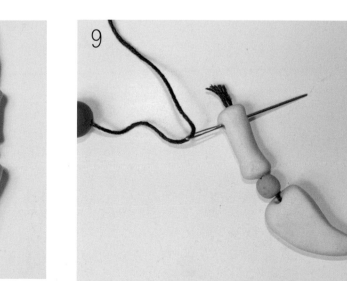

19

SPINY DINO CAPE

This dinosaur cape is quicker to make than saying "Micropachycephalosaurus"!
It is made from fleece, so feels nice and furry and goes with the paws on page 4.
You will need a sewing machine for this project.

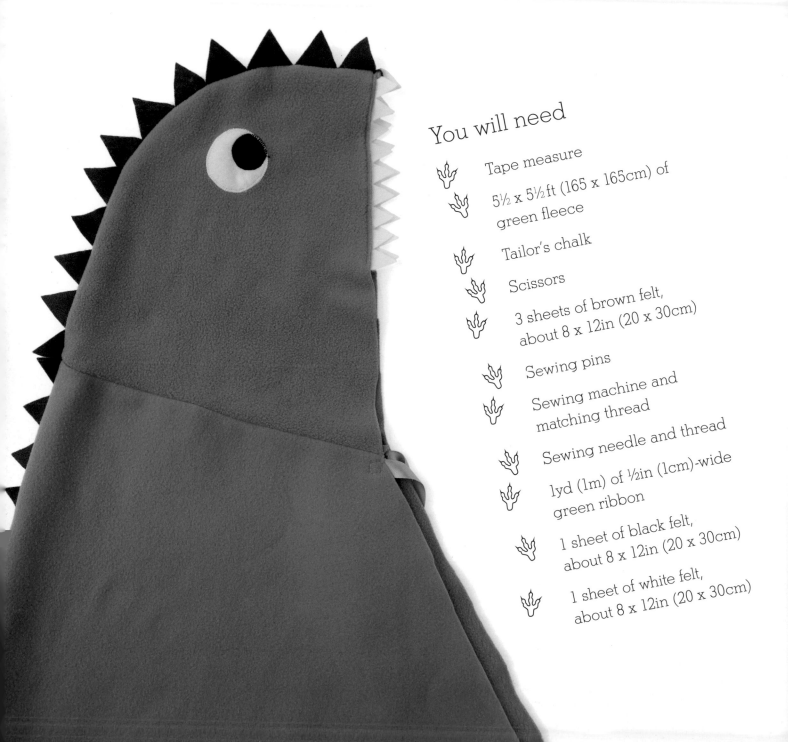

You will need

- Tape measure
- 5½ x 5½ ft (165 x 165cm) of green fleece
- Tailor's chalk
- Scissors
- 3 sheets of brown felt, about 8 x 12in (20 x 30cm)
- Sewing pins
- Sewing machine and matching thread
- Sewing needle and thread
- 1yd (1m) of ½in (1cm)-wide green ribbon
- 1 sheet of black felt, about 8 x 12in (20 x 30cm)
- 1 sheet of white felt, about 8 x 12in (20 x 30cm)

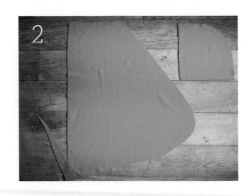

Step 1

Fold the fleece fabric in half. Use tailor's chalk to mark out the shapes of the hood and body, using the templates on the right as a guide for the measurements.

Step 2

Cut out two body pieces and two hood pieces from the fleece.

Step 3

Use the template on page 62 to cut out the spines from the brown felt. You will need around 15–20 spines to fill up the hood and body.

Step 4

Pin the spines facing inward along the curved edge of one of the hood pieces and the straight edge of one of the body pieces. Make sure the edges of the fabric all line up. Sew ¼in (5mm) from the edge to keep in place.

Step 5

Place the other body piece on top and pin the fabric together along the edge with spines. Sew with a ½in (1cm) seam allowance. Repeat for the hood piece.

Step 6

Open up the hood and cape. With the central seams lined up, pin the bottom of the hood to the top of the cape, right sides together, and sew with a ½in (1cm) seam allowance.

Step 7

Cut the ribbon in half and fold over each end twice by ½in (1cm) to conceal the raw edges. Pin onto each edge of the cape just under the join of the hood and body. Hand sew in place using matching thread.

Step 8

Use the template on page 62 to cut out two sets of eye pieces from the black and white felt. Sew the black part of the eye onto the white part around the edge of the black. Pin onto the hood of the cape approximately 3½in (9cm) from the front of the hood and 1½in (4cm) down from the spines. Sew in place and repeat for the other eye.

Step 9

Use the template on page 62 to cut out two sets of teeth from white felt. Pin on the inside of the hood, starting at the central seam and working outward. Trim the teeth to your preferred length and sew in place with a ¼in (5mm) seam allowance.

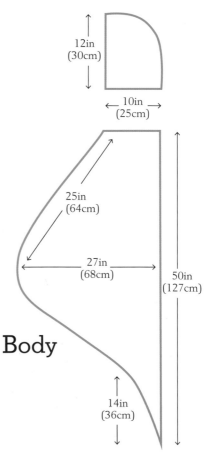

Hood

12in (30cm)

10in (25cm)

25in (64cm)

27in (68cm)

50in (127cm)

Body

14in (36cm)

4

5

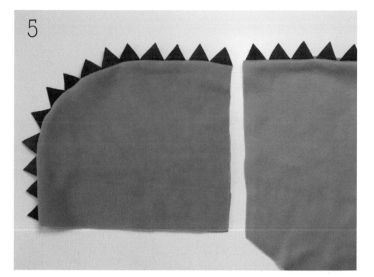

6

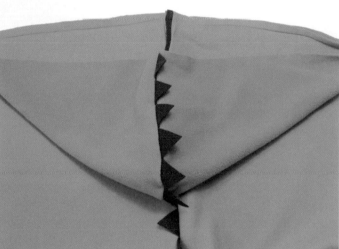

7

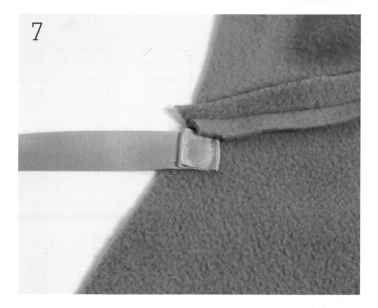

8

9

SNUGGLESAURUS CUSHION

Snugglesaurus is the cuddliest dinosaur around. He's really easy to make from fleece, flumped up nicely with stuffing to make him extra squishy. He has a handy pocket on his side for storing toys and books, or even a snack so he doesn't get hungry while you're snoozing! You will need a sewing machine to make this toy.

You will need

- 1 x 1½yd (1 x 1.5m) of blue fleece
- Scissors
- 3 sheets of green felt, about 8 x 12in (20 x 30cm)
- Sewing pins
- Sewing machine and matching thread
- 14oz (400g) bag of polyester fiber
- Large white button (1in/2cm diameter)
- Small black button (½in/1cm diameter)
- Sewing needle and thread

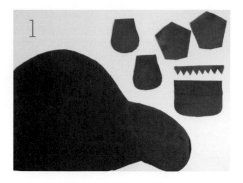

Step 1

Use the templates on page 63 to make the pattern pieces. You will need to cut two body pieces from the blue fleece to make each side of the dinosaur. Now cut four individual foot shapes and one pocket from the blue fleece, 10 individual spine shapes, and one pocket trimming from green felt.

Step 2

Pin two of the green spines together and sew around the edge with a ¼in (5mm) seam allowance. Repeat for the other spines. Neaten up the edges with scissors if necessary.

Step 3

Pin the pocket trimming along the top of the pocket and sew in place ¼in (5mm) from the edge.

Step 4

Pin the pocket into the middle of one of the body pieces and sew along the sides and bottom with a ¼in (5mm) seam allowance, keeping the top open.

Step 5

Pin and sew together two of the foot pieces with a ¼in (5mm) seam allowance, leaving the straight edge open. Repeat for the other foot.

Step 6

Turn the foot the right way out and stuff with a handful of polyester fiber. Repeat for the other foot.

Step 7

Pin the spines (evenly spaced) onto the pocketed body piece, along the top edge, pointing in. The raw edges of the felt and fleece should be lined up. Sew in place, with a ¼in (5mm) seam allowance, to secure.

Step 8

Pin and sew the feet facing upwards onto the bottom of the pocketed body piece, with the edges of the fabric lined up as before.

Step 9

Place the other body piece on top, right sides together, sandwiching in the spines and feet. Sew all around the cushion with a 1in (2.5cm) seam allowance, leaving 6in (15cm) open at the bottom for stuffing.

Step 10

Make snips into the seam to prevent puckering in the fabric. Turn the dinosaur the right way out, making sure all the corners are pushed out fully. Add polyester fiber so the cushion is nice and plump. Make small stitches along the opening at the bottom of the cushion to close.

Step 11

Place the black button onto the white button, position on the dinosaur's face and hand sew in place.

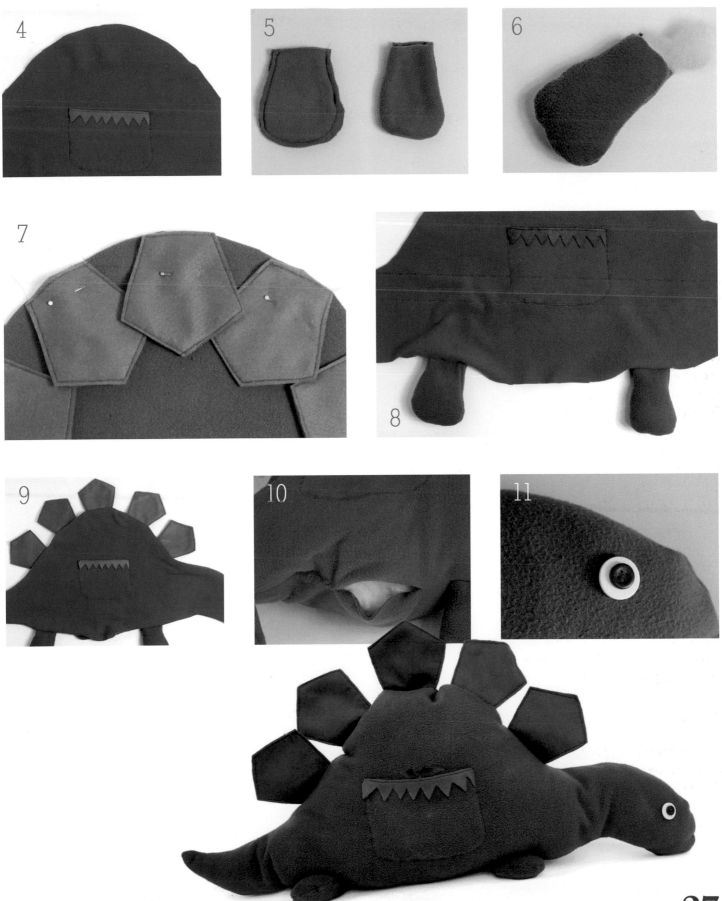

MINI JURASSIC LAND

The perfect place to play with toy dinosaurs, this land is really easy to make with some papier-mâché and paint. It also comes complete with a little cave under the volcano for your dinosaurs to sleep in. You can buy special model-making moss from craft stores and online, or hunt out your own from the garden. Collect interesting rocks, pebbles, and twigs that would look good in your little land.

You will need

 Scrap paper/newspaper for modeling

Masking tape

Cake board/hardboard measuring approximately 14in (36cm)

 PVA glue and water

 Gray, green, red, black, brown, blue, and yellow paint and paintbrushes

Scissors

 3 to 4 sheets of felt in different shades of green, about 8 x 12in (20 x 30cm)

Double-sided tape

 Pebbles, twigs, and moss

Scrap of red felt

Toy dinosaurs

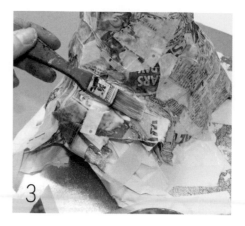

Step 1

To make the base of the volcano, scrunch up balls of paper and tape them onto the board to create a round base. Build up with more paper, beginning to form a cone shape.

Step 2

Twist paper into rings and tape to the top of the cone to form the crater of the volcano. Twist more paper and tape in layers at the bottom of the volcano to form a cave.

Step 3

Mix two parts glue to one part water to make papier-mâché paste. Use small bits of newspaper to cover the volcano and cave. Leave to dry overnight then add a second layer.

Step 4

Paint the volcano gray. Add a blue corner of sea with a yellow beach to the board, then paint the land green and leave to dry (you may need a couple of coats). For a textured effect use a sponge to apply paint to the land. Blend the colors a little to get a more natural looking landscape.

Step 5

Use a paintbrush to drop red and brown paint around the crater so that it dribbles down a little. If your paint is too thick, mix it with a little water first.

Step 6

For the bushes, cut a wavy strip from the length of a piece of green felt, about 3in (8cm) wide. Cut slits all the way down one side, as close together as you can, leaving 1in (2.5cm) uncut along the other side.

Step 7

Add a strip of double-sided tape along the uncut side of the felt. Cut the strip into four random segments. Unpeel the tape and roll the felt up to create a bush.

Step 8

From green felt, cut jagged shapes with a flat base to resemble ferns. Glue a small strip of red felt to the center.

Step 9

Glue the bushes and ferns onto the board along with some rocks, twigs, and moss. You can lay the twigs flat or glue them upright to look like trees. Use a little masking tape to hold them in place while the glue dries.

Step 10

Cut lots of little leaves from a mix of green felt and glue onto upright twigs to make them more treelike.

Step 11

Finally, add a slick of PVA glue to the lava and sea to give a bit of shine.

Step 12

When the glue is dry, your landscape will be ready to add dinosaurs.

4

5

6

7

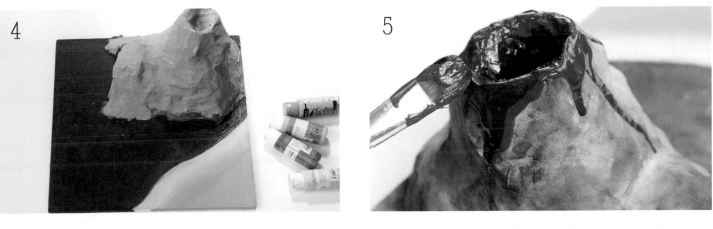

8

9

10

10

11

12

FOOTPRINT STAMPS

These super dinosaur feet stamps are easy to make and then fun to print with. Make a bunch of them in advance and put them out on the craft table at a dino party for an extra special printing activity.

You will need

- 1 sheet of craft foam, about 6 x 8in (15 x 21cm)

- Double-sided tape

- Scissors

- Corrugated card

- Duct tape

- Paints and paintbrushes or large stamp pad

Step 1

Use the templates provided on page 62 to create the shapes for your stamps. You can add more of your own, too. Bear in mind that the stamps work best if they are symmetrical, so create templates on a folded piece of paper and cut out. Draw around the templates onto the foam sheet.

Step 2

Cover the back of the foam with strips of double-sided tape.

Step 3

Cut out the stamps from the foam. Peel away the tape and stick them onto some corrugated card, making sure they are well spaced out.

Step 4

Cut around the corrugated card to cut out the stamps.

Step 5

Cut off 3in (7cm) lengths of duct tape. Pinch in the center to form a little handle, then stick onto the back of each stamp.

Step 6

Now you can print your dinosaur feet. There are several ways to do this: you can use a large stamp pad, press the feet onto a painted sponge, or paint the stamps using a brush.

Step 7

Now use the stamps to create your own prehistoric wrapping paper and cards.

PEG PUPPETS AND THEATER

This is a great craft for a rainy day. The puppets are made with pegs to enable them to open and close their mouths when pinched. We've used craft foam for the puppets as it is more durable, but you could also use colored card. Make a puppet theater to display your dinos so they can roar and chat away to each other.

You will need

- Scissors
- 6 sheets of craft foam in different colors, measuring approximately 6 x 8in (15 x 21cm), or colored card
- 6 wooden pegs
- White and black paint and paintbrushes
- Glue
- 6 googly eyes
- Paint in a variety of colors
- About 12 x 5in (30 x 12cm) fake grass (optional)
- String
- 1 sheet of green felt, about 8 x 12in (20 x 30cm)
- Large shoebox with removable lid

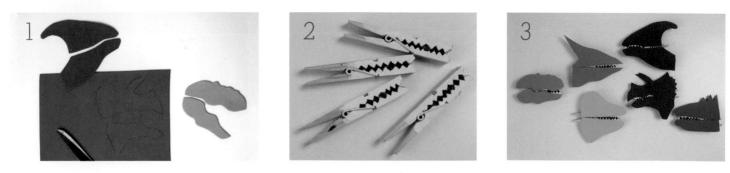

Step 1

Use the templates on page 63 to cut the shapes of the dinosaurs from different colors of craft foam (or cardboard if using). Each dinosaur has a bottom and a top piece.

Step 2

To make the teeth, paint the pegs white. You can leave the pinch end unpainted if you like. Leave to dry. Paint small triangles of black all along each inside edge of the peg.

Step 3

Line up one of the top foam pieces on one half of a peg so that it is at a slight angle to show a few teeth. Glue in place, making sure you can still pinch the peg open. Repeat for the bottom foam piece on the other half of the peg.

Step 4

Glue a googly eye onto each puppet.

Step 5

To make the prehistoric theater, draw a frame 1in (2.5cm) all the way around the lid of the box, then cut out the center. Repeat for the two small sides of the box, drawing and cutting out a ¾in (2cm) border. Paint the outside of the box and lid blue or any color you prefer.

Step 6

Paint the inside of the shoebox with a prehistoric scene; this will become the backdrop to your theater. Use the photo as a guide or design your own. Leave to dry.

Step 7

If you want, you can add grass to the theater by cutting fake grass to the same size as the long side of the box. Glue in place, underneath the backdrop.

Step 8

Glue the lid back in place. Make two holes for the curtain string on each side of the frame, about ¼in (5mm) from the top and front of the theater.

Step 9

For the curtains, cut the green felt in half across the width to create two panels. Mark every 1in (2.5cm) along the top and cut small holes at these points.

Step 10

Thread the curtains onto the string through the holes just cut in the felt. Thread through the holes in the side of the theater and tie to secure.

Step 11

Finally, cut palm leaf shapes from scraps of green craft foam (or card) and glue to the bottom of the frame. Add your dinos and let the Pantosaurus show begin!

You can create several backdrops for your theater. Simply draw around the bottom of the box onto a piece of card, decorate it, and attach it to the box with adhesive putty so that it can easily be changed.

TRICERATOPS PEN POT

What better way to store all your prehistoric writing implements than this colorful Triceratops pen pot! It is really easy to make from air-dry clay and corrugated card. Bear in mind the clay takes a couple of days to properly dry out, so you will need to do this project in two sessions.

You will need

- 2lb 3¼oz (1kg) air-dry clay
- Rolling pin
- Plastic wrap
- Scraps of corrugated card
- Scissors
- Masking tape
- Craft glue

- 2 cardboard tubes
- Craft knife
- Acrylic paint in your preferred colors and paintbrushes
- Pencil and thick permanent pen
- 2 googly eyes
- Craft varnish (optional)

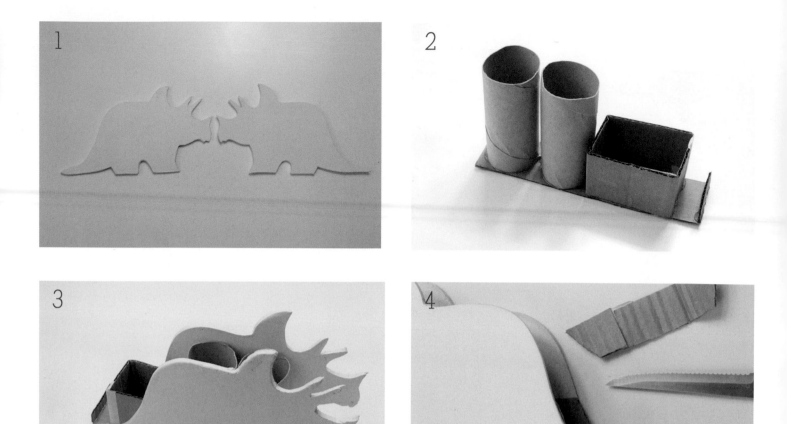

Step 1

Roll the clay to ¼in (5mm) thick between two pieces of plastic wrap. Use the template on page 63 to cut out two Triceratops shapes from the clay. They should be mirror images of each other. Use your fingers dipped in a little water to smooth the edges. Leave to dry for two days.

Step 2

Cut one strip of corrugated card measuring 2 x 10in (5 x 25cm), another measuring 2 x 7½in (5 x 19cm), and a tiny one measuring 2 x ½in (5 x 1cm). Fold the longest piece into a rectangle (2 x 3in/5 x 8cm) and tape to secure. Using the picture as a guide, glue the cardboard tubes and box onto the cardboard strip, then glue the small rectangle on the end, vertically. Leave to dry.

Step 3

Add glue to the sides of the tubes and cardboard and glue the Triceratops clay pieces onto the front and back.

Step 4

Use a craft knife to trim the corrugated box to fit more neatly with the lines of the Triceratops.

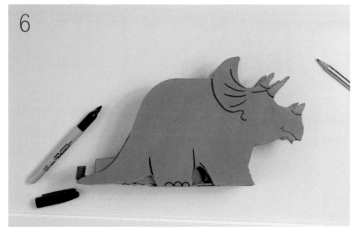

Rolling the clay out between sheets of plastic wrap allows you to easily see the thickness of the clay and prevents it from sticking to the rolling pin and the table.

Step 5

Paint the dinosaur and pots in contrasting colors using acrylic paints. Here we've gone for a nice bright purple for the Triceratops, and green for the inside of the pots. Leave to dry.

Step 6

Add details to your Triceratops in pencil—horn marks, toenails, and so on. Do not add eyes. Once you are happy with the design, go over the lines in thick permanent pen.

Step 7

Add more detail to the dinosaur by adding white horns, green toenails, and blue spots on his back. Glue on some googly eyes. If you like, you can add a layer of craft varnish to add strength and durability.

DINOSAUR HEAD MASK

Made from a shoebox, this fabulous T. rex head mask is perfect for stomping around the house in. It has an open mouth that acts as a visor to see out of. If you can't find upholstery foam to pad the inner mask, you could try cutting up dish sponges instead.

You will need

- Shoebox big enough to fit on your head
- Pen and scissors
- Scrap paper or newspaper
- Masking tape
- Newspaper
- PVA glue
- Green paint and paintbrush
- 1 sheet of white craft foam, about 8 x 12in (20 x 30cm)
- Scraps of black and green craft foam
- 30in (75cm) strip of 1in (2.5cm)-thick upholstery foam

Step 1

To form a rounded nose shape, turn the base of the shoebox upside down and draw curved edges onto one of the narrow ends. Open up that side of the box and cut slits up to the curve. Fold along the pen lines you drew and tape the box back together so that it has rounded corners.

Step 2

Scrunch up a ball of paper the same width as the box. Tape it to the bottom at the opposite end of the rounded nose, to create a head shape.

Step 3

Add more masking tape to smooth the paper into a more even shape.

Step 4

Scrunch two more pieces of paper to the size of a golf ball and tape to the rounded end to resemble nostrils. Add more tape to smooth as before.

Step 5

To make the dinosaur's jaw, cut most of the top off the lid so you are able to fit your head through the hole.

Step 6

Tape the lid onto the bottom of the box at an angle, to look like the mouth is open. Check the fit—you should be able to see out through the "mouth". Once you are happy with the angle, cover the whole box with papier-mâché. Mix two parts glue to one part water and use small bits of newspaper to cover the head. Leave to dry overnight, then add a second layer.

Step 7

Paint the head green, using several coats of paint.

Step 8

Add facial features. For the eyes, cut two ovals from white craft foam, measuring about 2½in (6cm). Cut another oval slightly bigger from green foam and cut this in half to create eyelids. Cut two small circles (about 1in/2.5cm) for the pupils and two arches (about 1½in/4cm) for the nostrils, from black foam. Glue onto the face as shown.

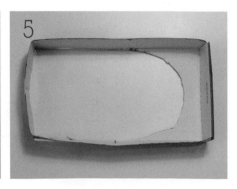

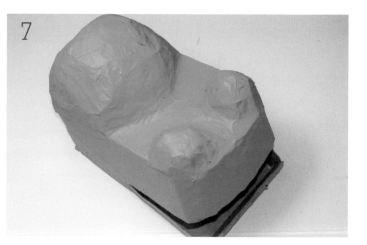

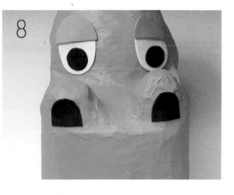

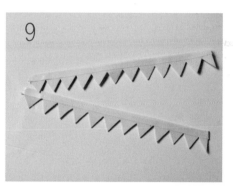

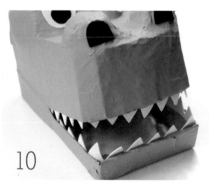

Step 9

Make the teeth by cutting zigzags along the length of a piece of white craft foam.

Step 10

Glue the teeth around the inside of the mouth on the top and bottom.

Step 11

Finally, push the piece of upholstery foam inside the box. Check the fit on the child and adjust the foam so that it is in the right position to hold the mask in place and add a little padding. When you are happy with the fit, glue the foam in place and trim the ends.

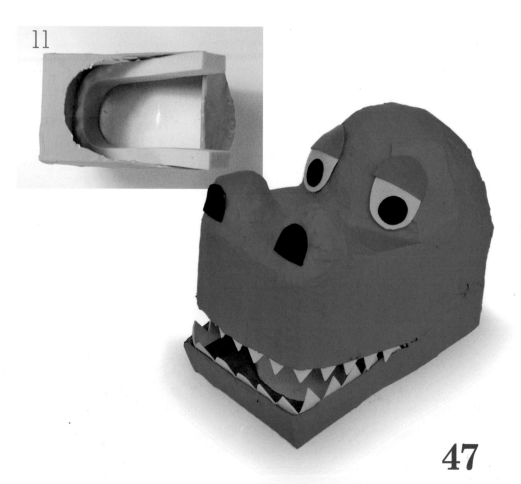

47

STRING AND NAIL ART

A must for the bedroom of any dinosaur fan, this T. rex string and nail art is fun to make. Adults should, of course, hammer the nails into the plywood, but kids can do the rest. Make your art look like ours, or create your own dino template for a more personalized finish.

You will need

- Sandpaper
- 12 x 12in (30 x 30cm) piece of plywood
- 1 sheet of plain paper, 8 x 12in (20 x 30cm)
- Sticky tape
- Hammer
- Approximately 70 nails
- Craft glue
- 2 reels of green sewing thread
- Glue
- Picture hanger

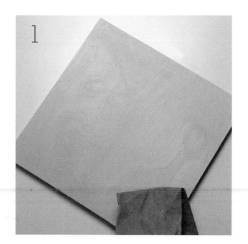

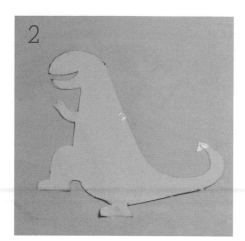

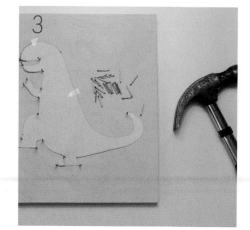

Step 1

Sand the plywood, if necessary, so that the wood is smooth and the edges softened.

Step 2

Copy and cut out the dinosaur template on page 64. Place it onto the board and tape it in place, centrally, with a little sticky tape.

Step 3

Hammer the first nail onto one of the corner points on the dinosaur, such as on the tail. Make sure the nail is straight and sturdy. Continue to hammer nails into each corner or angle on the dinosaur, to build the basic shape.

Step 4

Fill the outline with nails, spaced about ½in (1cm) apart.

Step 5

Remove the paper and tape to reveal a nailed outline of the dinosaur on the wood.

Step 6

With the thread still on the reel, wind it onto one of the nails and tie it in place. Pull the thread taut, wind it around the next nail along, then back to the first one. Now repeat to the next nearest nail, keeping the thread taut. Repeat going back and forth until you have threaded all the points within reach of the starting nail. You don't want to be bending the thread round any corners.

Step 7

Now pull the thread to the next nail and repeat the process. All the nails within reach of one another need to be connected for full coverage. If you want to come back to your art another time, use sticky tape to temporarily hold the thread to the board.

Step 8

Once the whole dinosaur shape is covered, finish loose ends by wrapping them onto a nail and adding a blob of glue to seal.

Step 9

Finally, glue a picture hanger to the back and leave to dry. Now you can hang your art on your bedroom wall.

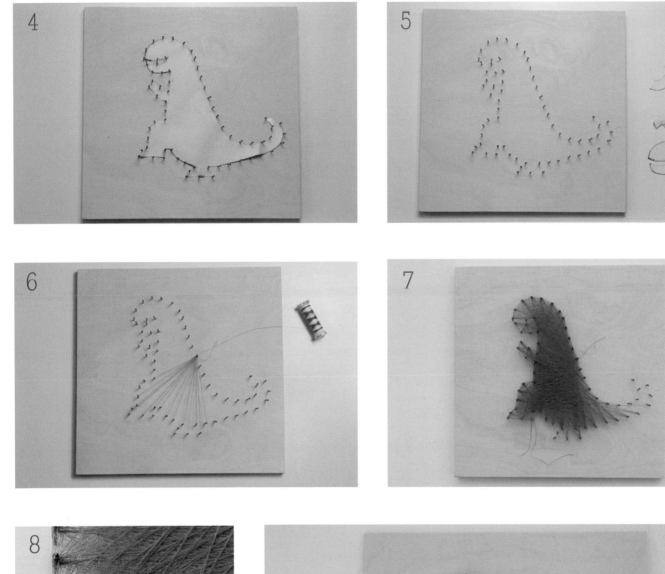

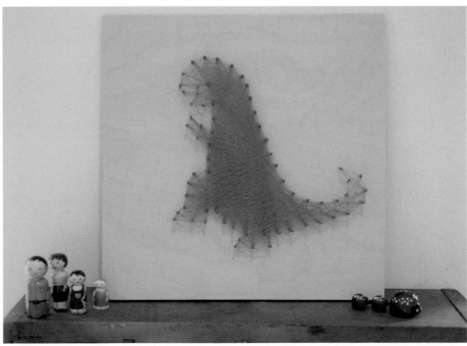

MAGNETIC PENCIL CASE

This lovely little pencil case doubles as a mini dinosaur play scene, making it perfect for bored kids when you're traveling. We have provided templates for the magnets, but you might find it fun to create your own. Acrylic paints are best for a good coverage and durability, so cover up clothes and surfaces before painting!

You will need

 Scissors

 2 sheets of shrink plastic, 8 x 12in (20 x 30cm)

Acrylic paints and paintbrushes

Selection of colored permanent marker pens

Craft varnish

Strong glue

5 small magnets

Adhesive putty, such as Blu Tack

 Old metal pencil case

Step 1

Use the templates provided on page 63 to create dinosaur shapes, or design your own. Remember that the templates need to be around 5–6in (12–15cm) wide to start with as the plastic will shrink a lot in the oven.

Step 2

Draw around the templates onto shrink plastic and cut out. Place on a baking tray.

Step 3

Follow the manufacturer's instructions to shrink the plastic dinosaur shapes in the oven. They will only take a few minutes and will curl up before resettling at around a tenth of their original size. Do not remove them from the oven until they are flat.

Step 4

Once shrunk, paint the dinosaurs in whatever colors you choose. You may need several coats for a good coverage.

Step 5

Add features using colored permanent marker pens, then give a slick of varnish to finish. Leave to dry.

Step 6

Flip the dinosaurs over and glue the magnets onto the back.

Step 7

For the base coat of the pencil case, paint the outside of the lid in your preferred color. Use several coats to cover up any designs underneath. Leave to dry. To create the silhouette, cut out one of the templates for the shrink plastic and use adhesive putty to stick it onto the center of the lid, using lots of tiny bits to ensure there are no gaps. Paint the lid and base of the pencil case in a contrasting color. Hold the brush upright and dab paint on gently to avoid it creeping under the template. Peel away the template to reveal the silhouette below.

Step 8

Paint the inside of the pencil case lid with a Jurassic scene. You could add volcanoes, palm trees, waterfalls, and rivers. Leave to dry, then add a coat of varnish to the pencil case on both the inside and outside—this will stop the paint from being scratched.

Step 9

Once dry, you can add your magnetic dinosaurs to the pencil case and you are good to go.

3

4

5

6
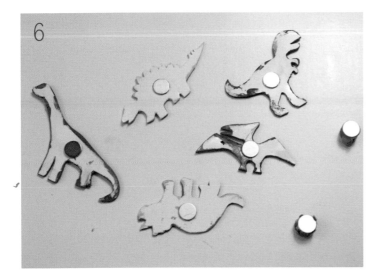

7

8

9

PARTY-SAURUS

Throwing a prehistoric party is really easy with the help of our handy guide. Here are some useful ideas for dinosaur-themed party food, games, and decor. For the perfect centerpiece, turn to page 58 for how to make an explosive Volcano Cake.

FOOD

Pterodactyl nests
Create simple nests by mixing melted chocolate with broken up shredded wheat cereal. Shape into nests, add some chocolate eggs, and top with a toy dinosaur, then pop in the fridge to set. Be sure that the toy is large enough not to be a choking hazard.

Fossil cookies
Cut circular cookies and use small plastic dinosaurs to print dino bodies and feet into the dough before baking.

Dino sandwiches
Either use dinosaur or footprint cookie cutters to create really simple dino sandwiches that kids will love. Or cut sandwiches into triangles and label them "dino spikes."

Dinosaur bones
Make a batch of cheese straws. Cut them into strips, then mold each end into a bone shape before baking.

Dinosaur juice
Blend a few bunches of spinach with a little orange juice to make a deep green paste, then mix with more orange juice to create beautiful green dino juice with hidden healthiness!

DECORATION

Footprints
Cut giant dino footprints from card to lead partygoers to the fun.

Dinosaur hats
Make a set of party hats by cutting card into semicircles, bending them into cones, and securing with double-sided tape. Add card spines down the back and elastic to keep it in place.

Table decorations
A green tablecloth will turn your table into a mini Jurassic land which you can decorate with toy dinosaurs, trees, and moss. Add "carnivore" or "herbivore" labels and put out green food (such as cucumber or bell peppers) in pots so it looks like the table is full of shrubbery. Cut out dinosaur silhouettes for place settings and add pots of crayons so kids can decorate them while they wait to eat.

Party bags
Decorate paper bags with a footprint or dinosaur silhouette and add each child's name on a bone-shape label. Fill with things like dinosaur chocolate eggs, the footprint stamps from page 32, dinosaur-shape crayons (which you can make by melting old crayons into a silicone mold), and stickers. Have an "adopt a dinosaur" basket near the exit with a selection of dinosaurs labeled with silly names for children to select on their way out.

PARTY GAMES

Dino dig treasure hunts
Hide mini plastic dinosaurs or the fossils from page 12 and send your little paleontologists on a hunt for them. Or arm them with mini shovels to see how many they can dig from a sandbox.

Hunt the T. rex
Cut a large T. rex silhouette from different colored card for each child or team. Cut the shape into segments, like a jigsaw, and hide around the house. The winner is the one who pieces together their dinosaur first.

Craft tables
Have sheets of paper out with the stamps from page 32 or make dinosaur-spotter binoculars by taping two small cardboard tubes together and decorating with pens, stickers, and glitter. They will come in handy for the Hunt the T. rex game above.

VOLCANO CAKE

If you want a showstopper for your prehistoric party, try this explosive cake!
Team it with the party food ideas on page 57 for a feast no dinosaur will want
to miss. Steps 1 and 2 can be done in advance if you have room in your freezer.

You will need

For the cake:

- 1lb 5oz (600g) superfine/caster sugar
- 1lb 5oz (600g) self-rising flour
- 12 eggs
- A few drops of vanilla extract
- 5 tsp baking powder

For the buttercream frosting:

- 12oz (350g) softened butter
- 1lb 9oz (700g) confectioner's/icing sugar
- 4 tbsp milk
- 12 drops of vanilla extract

To decorate:

- 3½oz (100g) jelly/jam
- 1lb 2oz (500g) brown ready-to-use fondant
- 3½oz (100g) green ready-to-use fondant
- 1¾oz (50g) cocoa puffed rice cereal
- 8oz (225g) white chocolate
- Red, green, and black food coloring
- 1 tbsp confectioner's/icing sugar
- 5oz (150g) dry, unsweetened coconut
- Ice fountain candle (optional)
- 15oz (425g) chocolate finger cookies
- Small plastic dinosaur animals

Supplies:

- 2 x 9in (23cm) cake pans
- 18fl oz (500ml) Pyrex bowl
- Knife
- 2in (5cm) round cookie cutter
- 2in (5cm) scrap of paper
- 11in (28cm) cake board

Step 1

Preheat the oven to 350°F (180°C). Grease and line the two cake pans and grease the Pyrex bowl. Cream the butter and sugar together. When they are smooth and creamy, mix in the eggs along with the vanilla extract. Sift the flour and baking powder together and fold in. Pour the mixture into the bowl until it is two-thirds full, then divide the remaining mixture between the two pans. Bake the three cakes in the oven for 30–40 minutes or until they are golden brown.

Step 2

Make the buttercream by mixing all the ingredients together. Spread a layer of buttercream and jelly onto one of the large cakes and sandwich together.

Step 3

Use a knife to cut the domed cake to form more of a pointed shape to resemble a volcano (keep hold of the offcuts for the next step). Use the cookie cutter to cut a round crater out of the center. Push it all the way to the bottom. At this point you can freeze the cakes, if required.

Step 4

Cover the large cake with a layer of buttercream and place the volcano on top. Place the offcuts of cake around the base of the volcano to create a smooth shape and cover with buttercream.

Step 5

Roll out the brown fondant until it is wide enough to cover the volcano. Gently place it on top and let it form natural folds to resemble a volcano. Cut off the excess fondant around the base of the volcano. Cut into the crater and open it up.

Step 6

Mix approximately ½ teaspoon of green food coloring with 1½ tablespoons (25ml) water. Pour over the coconut and mix together to turn the coconut green. Sprinkle around the volcano on the cake.

Step 7

Cut a small palm leaf template from a scrap of paper. Roll out the green fondant and use the template to cut six leaves.

Step 8

Mix 1 tablespoon of confectioner's sugar with a little egg white to form a gluey paste. Arrange three of the leaves with the ends overlapping in the middle and glue together with the paste. Roll a small ball of fondant; dip the end of a chocolate finger cookie into the paste and press into the ball. Add a dab of the paste onto the center of the leaves and press the ball and cookie onto the leaves. Leave upside down to harden overnight.

Step 9

Melt 2½oz (75g) of white chocolate and add a few drops of red food coloring to create a rich red lava color. Pour around the crater and let it drip down the sides. Let the chocolate harden.

Step 10

Place the chocolate finger cookies vertically around the base of the cake.

Step 11

Melt the remaining white chocolate and mix with black food coloring to create a rocky gray color. Mix the cocoa puffed rice into the mixture then into different sized clumps to create bolders. Place some of these onto the cake and reserve the rest for serving as party food.

Step 12

Add the palm trees and some small plastic dinosaurs onto to the cake. If you like, you can pop a fountain candle into the volcano to create an exciting erupting effect.

TEMPLATES

The templates that are 100% can be traced and cut out, or photocopied. Other templates will need to be enlarged on a photocopier to the percentage stated. Align each template as near to the top left-hand corner of the photocopier glass as possible. You may need to repeat this a few times to find the best position.

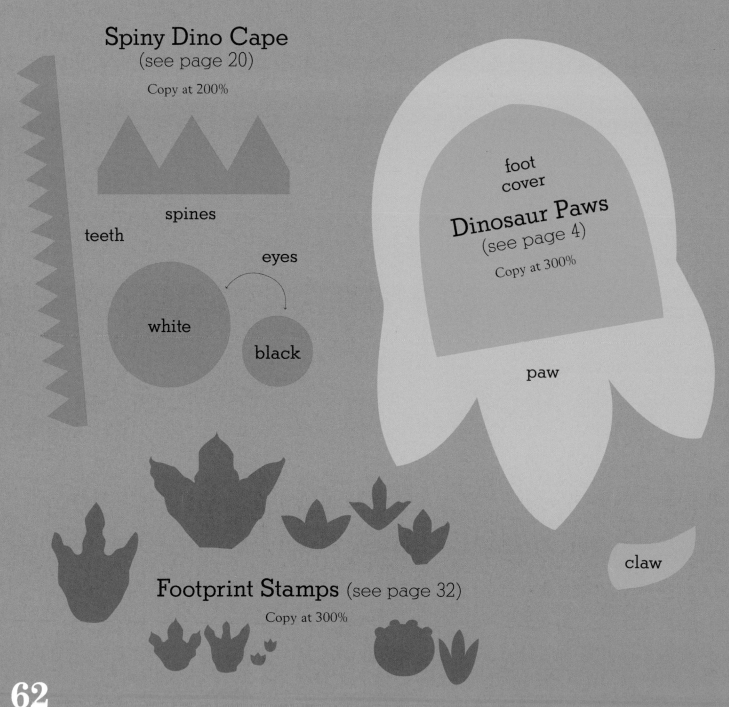

Spiny Dino Cape
(see page 20)

Copy at 200%

spines

teeth

eyes

white

black

foot cover

Dinosaur Paws
(see page 4)

Copy at 300%

paw

claw

Footprint Stamps (see page 32)

Copy at 300%

Stegosaurus

Brachiosaurus

Pterodactyl

Triceratops Pen Pot
(see page 40)
Copy at 200%

Magnetic Pencil Case
(see page 52)

Copy at 150%

Triceratops

Tyrannosaurus

feet

spines

body

pocket

Snugglesaurus Cushion
(see page 24)

Copy at 600%

trimming

Peg Puppets and Theater (see page 36)

Copy at 200%

Pterodactyl

Triceratops   Parasaurolophus   Tyrannosaurus   Stegosaurus   Pachycephalosaurus

String and Nail Art
(see page 48)

Copy at 100%